Prison Days

Book 6

True Diary Entries
by a Maximum-Security Prison Officer

November, 2018

By Simon King

Prison Days June

Prison Days July

Prison Days August

Prison Days September

Prison Days October

Prison Days- The First Four Months

The Final Alibi
(The Ploughman Chronicles Book 1)

COMING SOON

Prison Days: Inmates

MAX
(Book 1)

Introduction

Welcome to yet another month of Prison Days. As I'm sitting here and pondering just where this series has already taken me, and you for that matter, I truly am comforted in knowing that there isn't a shortage of material that inmates provide me. What I mean is, the events that happen on a daily basis are so varied and intriguing that I could continue to write for a very long time and not run out of subject matter.

Just look at the last hour for example. I'm sitting here in Goulburn West on night shift and it's an hour and a half after lockdown. There have been 2 code mikes already, including one from this unit where a prisoner had shoved a pen into his rectum and made it bleed. He's an IDS prisoner and needs to be kept separated from other prisoners due to his vulnerability.

When I asked him why he jammed a pen into his butt, he said that he felt horny. That prisoner has been shoving things into his anus for as long as I have been a guard and does what he does for attention. The reason, like so many of his kind, is that they have a need to be the centre of attention in order to feel liked. They do this through slashing up, bronzing up, faking suicide and yes, jamming things where there is no logical reason to jam them. It takes up a lot of resources but unfortunately cannot be avoided.

My point is, despite initially believing this series to continue for two or three books, its' now into its sixth, and as long as you, the reader, continue reading them, I am happy to continue writing them for you.

I do have one thing I wanted to share with you. When I first began to write these books, fellow authors advised me not to read reviews, as some may not always be favourable. I do read them though and I thank everyone who has written me one because they do really mean a lot. They were right in that not everyone will be as entertained by these books as most have been and that's OK. That's what makes reading so interesting. If you knew you were going to love each and every book you ever picked up, then there wouldn't be any mystery.

But one of these 1-star reviews stated that my books read like a diary and lacked the emotional side of how these events affect me. The point I wanted to make was that that is exactly what I am aiming for; a real, unbiased look at life behind bars without too much influence from my own feelings and emotions. A true-to-life glimpse into the world beyond the walls so to speak. And that way, I hand the decision on whether something is fair, evil, crazy, cold-blooded or just downright wrong to you, the reader. Make your own mind up about these events and share your thoughts with me on my Facebook page.

But for now, let's not worry what others think. Let's focus on the road ahead as we delve into another month of the unpredictable experiences that are maximum security.

Units

All the units in the prison are named after rivers and consist of management, step-down management, protection and main stream.

Management Units

Units that are predominately single occupancy out of necessity or punishment and have 23-hour lock ins. Prisoners only receive a one hour run out from their cell.
Murray North and South are the Management Units.

Step Down Management

Units that are a step down from the 23-hour lock down. Prisoners are given extra run-outs throughout the day but limited to around 3 to 4 hours. Some prisoners can mix and have joint run-outs.
Goulburn East and West are the Step-Down Management Units.

Protection Units

Yarra North and South, Loddon North and South, Glenelg East and West

Main Stream Units

Thomson East and West, Tambo East and West, Campaspe, Avoca, Maribyrnong,

Other Areas

Kitchen, Laundry, Medical Wing, Reception

Some Prison Terms

- Air- Raiding- Yelling or abusing someone loudly in the middle of a unit.

- Billet- A prisoner who is assigned a particular duty in the unit, on a daily basis, for a weekly pay packet. They hold the position until they are either transferred out, sacked or quit.

- Bone Yard- A protection unit. Protection prisoners are also known as Boners.

- Booted- To hide something in the anus

- Boss- What prisoners call an officer. It began early last century, is a reverse insult and means "Sorry Son of a Bitch"

- Brew- A cup of Coffee or Tea

- Brasco- Toilet or brasco roll is toilet paper.

- Bronze Up- To cover ones' self in faeces.

- Bunk- A prisoner's bed.

- Burning- Prisoners abusing a crook or officer for an extended period of time.

- Canteen- A prisoner's weekly shopping or shopping items.

- Cellie- A cellmate

- Chook Pen- A fenced-in area attached to a unit for prisoners to walk around in. Approximately 15m by 15m depending on which unit. Management units have multiple chook pens as prisoners have individual run outs throughout the day.

- Co-ee- A prisoner's co-accused

- Crook- How officers refer to inmates

- Dog- Someone who informs on another prisoner.

- Greens or Greys- Prisoner's prison uniform.

- Rock Spider- A paedophile.

- Screw- How inmates refer to officers.

- Shiv- home-made knife or blade.

- Slash Up- To self-harm

- The T.O.'s- Tactical Officers, that are highly trained and armed with batons and O.C. spray.

- Trap- A small latch in a cell door that can be lowered to allow access. It is normally either half way up or three quarters of the way up the cell door.

Codes

- Alpha- Officer needs assistance, Officer emergency

- Bravo- Lock down of Unit

- Charlie- Lock down of prison

- Delta- Fire

- Echo- Escape

- Foxtrot- Fight, Prisoner on Prisoner

- Mike- Medical emergency

I was stationed in Thomson West for the first of 2 shifts, as one of the regular officers was away on annual leave for a week. I've never minded working in this particular unit as the officers allocated here permanently are a pretty good bunch. Most of the crooks were OK too, definitely unlike several other units that were generally filled with the "needy" kind.

For some reason I felt off, coming in for the first shift today. I put it down to just something in the air but I had the never-ending feeling of the day ahead going pear-shaped even before setting foot inside the walls.

My two offsiders for this shift were both brand new, barely a couple of weeks out from their training course. Meagan Henry was an overly-enthusiastic pleaser that seemed to have a genuine need to see everyone content before she'd sit down, while David Tansy was the exact opposite; a lazy couldn't-be-bothered kind of guy that favoured sitting in the station rather than actively participating in running the unit.

I'm not one to judge anyone but being brand new and already lazy with a need to kick back at every opportunity puts the onus on me to set him straight and frankly, I spend enough time needing to set crooks straight without an officer adding to it.

Meagan already has the muster sheet in hand when control calls for count and I follow her around the unit, dropping traps and calling out numbers to her. It doesn't take long for us to add up our tally and call it through. Once control calls count correct, I head to the top deck, while Meagan unlocks the bottom cells, the units' 72 prisoners scrambling for the toasters.

As I step back into the officer's station, the intercom buzzes and David answers the call, listening as a prisoner complains of feeling dizzy. His cell is on the bottom tier and I head over to it to check it out.

The crook is still lying in his bunk when I open his door, not looking well.

"What's up, Jeffery?" I ask and he peers up at me with squinting eyes. I can see he's quite sweaty despite it feeling fresh and he struggles up onto his elbow.

"My head feels all weird," he replies, then without warning, vomits across himself, the retching sounding like gravel in his throat. The rancid stink is almost instant and I have no choice but to call a code mike. Meagan is standing behind me with her radio turned up to almost maximum, the call shouting across the unit. There's a definite groan as everyone is aware of what happens next.

Because a code mike requires the medical staff to attend the unit, they won't enter until all the prisoners are locked away, meaning we have to lock everyone down immediately. I stick my head out of the cell and call out to David who's still sitting in the station.

"Lock 'em down," I call out and with a unified groan, prisoners head back to their cells, some scrambling for bits of bread and other necessities. Others are quickly setting up the washing machines and David looks timid as he tries to get the crooks to move back to their cells. I turn to Meagan and whisper for her to return to the station and announce it over the unit PA as Jeffery launches into another bout of retching.

The nurses are waiting outside the unit within a few minutes as we lock the remaining few prisoners away. Once we finish, Meagan opens the door for them and they wheel their trolley to Jeffery's cell where he's still fighting to get his stomach under control. Several of the prisoners begin to cheer as the nurses enter but it has nothing to do with them. The nurses are both male and the cheering has more to do with the fact that they've finally made it to the cell, the unit wanting to be released so as to continue with morning routines.

As the nurses do what they need to with several officers standing close to ensure their safety, I return to the station and begin typing out my report for calling the code. It's only a few lines of text, stating the main points of the incident. It's only a minor code mike and doesn't require anything too extravagant.

Just as I print it out for the supervisor, a stretcher enters the unit and is taken to Jeffery's cell. He's deemed too unwell to remain and will be wheeled down to the prison's hospital wing. Once there, the nurses will determine if he'll require an ambulance for transport to hospital or simply a bed within the unit there. Either way, he'll be taken out of here for the time being.

We stand by while Jeffery is helped onto the stretcher and once he and the nurses have exited the unit, begin to unlock it for a second time. Most of the crooks thank me as I unlock the top tier and once done, return to the station.

Within a few minutes, the medical trolley arrives and I ask David to help the trolley's accompanying officer with regulating the medicinal dispersion, one officer needed to visually confirm consumption of pills and potions by checking mouths as they finish with the pill room. He actually groans as he stands to go and it tickles me in just the right place.

"Excuse me? Is there a problem with you doing your job?" I ask, Meagan turning to watch. He mumbles something under his breath but heads for the now already forming line by the closed door of the pill room. I look at Meagan and she just shakes her head.

"He was like that on the course as well," she said and now it's my turn to groan.

As the medication line begins to dwindle, I prep the movement slips for those prisoners who are about to head off to morning classes. The prison runs many courses which the prisoners have access to, most creating opportunities with which to better themselves and increase their chances of finding work once back out in the community.

Unfortunately, they are also seen by many as an easy way to increase the chance for parole, never actually wanting the qualifications for what they were intended for but rather a tool to be used when attending court.

But just as I'm about to call for the required prisoners, there's a commotion behind me and when I turn, see a prisoner tumble down the steel staircase. There's no-one else nearby and Meagan is already on her radio to call another code as the prisoner is lying at the foot of the stairs, crying in agony. His left leg is positioned precariously away from him and it doesn't take a second look to tell that it's broken.

I don't need to tell you the response from the prisoners as I make the call for the unit to be locked down yet again. They aren't happy but know that we have little choice so don't give us too much of a hard time.

"Fuck you, cunts," is suddenly screamed from behind me and I turn to see one of the unit billets standing on the top tier.

"What are you doing?" someone yells from the other end of the unit and I see that the billet has an extension cord in his hands. He's the person that does the vacuuming of the unit's carpeted areas and thus has access to the vacuum and necessary extension leads that are needed. He's now holding one of them in his hands, one end tied around his neck and the other end about to be tied to the railing.

"Scott!" I call, trying to get his attention. I see Meagan on the phone and assume it's to control, requesting a second code and asking for back-up.

"Shut up, Boss," he said to me. "I'm not doing this shit for another 20 fucking years." He's crying, snot hanging from his nose as he ties the lead off. Some of the other prisoners are cheering, a couple laughing and this just sets him off some more. "Yeah, fucking laugh about it. I'm sick of this shit," he screams.

I probably need to point out to you, (again if you've been on this ride since the beginning or for the first time if this is your initial entry point to Prison Days,) but some prisoners aren't the brightest sparklers in the sky. Not to say that some of our residents aren't teetering on the edge of genius, but unfortunately for others, not so much.

What followed in the next 5 or so seconds could be put down to either not thinking the entire process through due to the stress of the situation, forgetting some very appropriate and fitting physics lessons or just a simple brain fart.

Scott climbed the railing, precariously balanced on the top one for maybe a second or two, closed his eyes and then calmly said "Later Motherfuckers," before stepping off and plunging into the abyss below. In his mind he may have visualized a scene where he plunged to his death to the gasps of surprised crooks, maybe even shouts of astonishment at his fearless and courageous act.

What actually transpired was that the extension cord which was wrapped around his neck had not been measured correctly. Not only did he reach the end of the proverbial rope only an inch or two above the ground, but his would-be hangman's rope snapped due to the weight difference between the maximum break point of the cord and our unfortunate victim's body weight. He struck the very hard and robust concrete floor with both feet at the same time, snapping both legs in various spots, including one unfortunate shard that now stuck out from his pants in a bloody and grotesque manner. Our would-be-suicide-person was squirming about on the floor as a mixture of shock, pain and embarrassment washed across his white face. The unit exploded into a chorus of laughter, cheers and finger pointing as they howled with delight, drowning out the cries of agony.

Prison isn't really the place for pity and our unfortunate prisoner received none, looking at us officers for escape from the torment. Meagan was still on the phone and I could see her now talking frantically into it. I have no doubt that control was already aware of the situation, in all likelihood witnessing the entire sequence on their monitors.

It doesn't take long for the officers to stream back into the unit, most helping to lock it down. Although it's another disruption to their morning routine, the prisoners seem unfazed at being returned to their cells yet again, most still laughing at the unfortunate soul lying on the floor.

Once the unit is completely locked down, the nurses enter together with a stretcher. But if you think that's the end of the apathetic abuse from the prisoners then you would be mistaken. There are enough gaps and cracks between their cell doors and adjoining walls to ensure none miss out on the show. The goading continues throughout the nurse's assessment and subsequent treatment and hits a fever pitch crescendo as Scott is wheeled out on the stretcher still groaning with pain.

It's another report I need to write and get to it while the nurses are leaving through the airlock, two officers pushing the stretcher for them. By the time the unit is unlocked again, I'm pressing send on my email, the reports finished and on its way to the duty sup.

A number of prisoners make their way to the officer's station, still animated with the 'excitement' of the morning so far.

"Boss, can we go to the gym?" one asks and I phone the gym for confirmation. After confirming that it's OK, I write each of the crooks a movement slip and send them on their way. I also continue with the education slips and once finished, call the appropriate recipients up to collect them. Once the twenty-two leave the unit, there's an instant calm that descends over it, voices only distant murmurs as everyone quietly goes about their daily routine.

With almost 40 prisoners less, tasks become so much easier and I ask David to check that morning's random cell search list. I figure it better to complete them whilst half the unit is out, needing to leave a single officer in the station. As I wait for the list, I consider my options for who to take with me to conduct the searches. I know that Meagan is keen to learn and would jump at the chance, but I also see her as the more confident of the 2, predicting her to be more capable of handling herself if confronted in the station by crooks. David, on the other hand, needs to be kept busy, the one more likely to fall asleep whilst manning the station alone.

"Do you mind holding the fort while we go do the searches?" I ask her and Meagan nods, watching as her demeanour grows in confidence at running the show for a bit. A good side-effect of leaving Meagan in the station alone is that she will be tested by prisoners keen to see whether she's able to be 'bought' or intimidated. Taking advantage of an officer isn't anything new and can be quite confronting and it's probably best for her to experience it early in her career.

"All under control," she said, shooting us a 2-thumbs-up. I wave for David to follow me and make my way to the first cell, a single-outer on the bottom tier. The prisoner is sitting on his bunk reading a book and isn't too fussed when we interrupt him. I wave for David to take the lead and he conducts the strip search, finding nothing of interest.

"Anything in here that shouldn't be?" I ask and the prisoner shakes his head. Once he exits, I close the door and we begin searching.

10 minutes is all it takes to go through everything, finding nothing of interest to us. The crook salutes us comically as we emerge and resumes his novel, something by Stephen King. I close the door and head to the next cell, located up on the second tier. David is grumbling about something as we climbed the stairs.

"Something the matter?" I asked as I reached the top.

"No," was all he managed, looking at the stairs as he climbed. I wasn't sure what the issue was but assumed he really didn't want to be doing anything other than sitting on his butt. We reached the second cell and found it locked. The occupant was one of the "gym" crooks and so we entered without too much of an issue, commencing our search immediately.

Other than a single picture of a naked woman, torn from a magazine, the cell was clean. I crumpled the picture up and put it in my pocket, keeping it for disposal once back in the station. Although technically contraband, it didn't really warrant any subsequent disciplinary action other than a caution upon the occupant's return.

The third cell we search provides a slightly better result as David locates a toothbrush shiv hidden inside the stuffing of the pillow, as well as a single pill which was left sitting on the window sill. Complacency goes both ways, with prisoners sometimes forgetting where they are.

Much to David's disgust, it's up to him to write the report, which he does once we return to the station. I'm amazed by the attitude but know it's none of my business. As long as he continues to do as he's asked, regardless of the mutterings, then I'm happy.

Just as lunchtime count is called over the radio, there's an influx of returning prisoners from the gym. The airlock is filled a number of times as they make their way back inside and head straight to their cells, eyeing the kitchen billets busily preparing their meals as they pass. Once they are all back inside, Meagan announces muster over the unit P.A. system and we conduct count in relative silence.

Meagan takes the clipboard and walks along the cells as David and I take position in the middle of the unit to conduct our own count. I watch as she slowly marks names of, peering into each cell to ensure its occupant is out. Once she's traversed both levels and returns to the station, I yell for the unit to break off and everyone makes a beeline for the kitchen, plates in hand.

Once all 3 of us are happy that our numbers match, Meagan calls it into control and a few minutes later are relieved to hear it called correct, signalling the beginning of the afternoon. It's great to be able to just sit and relax after the morning's incidents, the attempted suicide still the talk of the unit.

I listen to a group of prisoners who are sitting near us talking about it, laughing as one describes the look on the unfortunate Scott's face as he hit the floor. Others soon join in the laughter as they eat, visibly enjoying recollections from different angles. All I can think is that if they are laughing together then they aren't arguing and that's a good thing for us.

I phone the supervisor for a quick chat and find out that Scott had been taken straight to the hospital via ambulance, something I suspected but wanted to confirm. Knowing if a prisoner was returning to the unit is good knowledge to have when it came time for final lockdown.

Once the meals are finished, the afternoon dissolves into several different activities across the unit. There's a game of pool here, several prisoners vying for "unit champion" of table tennis over there, as well as several card games. A game of chess is started near us by two older prisoners and I watch as they silently go about trying to outwit each other over the course of a couple of hours.

About an hour before lockdown, just as the med trolley pulls into the unit for the final time, I come to realise that one particular prisoner is still actively talking about Scott. It strikes me as odd as the laughter around the subject had died off considerably throughout the afternoon, yet he continued to try and drum up an audience with his vocalized story-telling.

As Meagan heads to the airlock to help with the dispensing of the medication, the phone rings. I answer it and listen as the sup asks for a particular crook to be watched until the Tactical boys come to grab him. The prisoner he mentions is called James Dobbs and just happens to be the one still wanting to go on about Scott.

The sup advises me that Scott had made some allegations against James and after reviewing camera footage of the unit, determined there to be sufficient cause for a formal interview with the prisoner. He doesn't elaborate on what the allegations are, other than to say it looked as if Scott had been stood over.

James doesn't argue as the Tactical boys arrive, accompanying them out of the unit. There's a murmur amongst the other prisoners as he is led out but it dies down quickly once he's disappeared out of the airlock.

He doesn't return by the time we lock the unit down for the night, remaining up in one of the admission buildings whilst interviewed by police. As I walk out, I'm glad that the first day of the month is over, but feel a faint flicker in the pit of my stomach about what the rest of the month had in store. I thank my offsiders as we re-enter the outside world and breathe easier once safely back in my car. Today has been an OK day.

Friday, November 2

As I enter the unit for day 2 of my 3-day stretch, I'm happy to see Meagan already in the station going over the muster.

Hey," she calls out as I come through the airlock and I return her wave. "James got taken out of the unit. See? Not on here," she said, holding the muster up. I look and see that his name has been removed. When I check the movement log for the previous day, I point out that he'd been moved to one of the management units.

"Probably found that he'd been doing naughty stuff," Meagan said as I put my bag away.

It doesn't take me long to find out the details of what had transpired the night before, thanks to a quick call to the sup. It turns out that James had not only been standing over Scott but also his girlfriend on the outside, courtesy of another prisoner's brother. The brother had been visiting Scott's girlfriend on a number of occasions, trying to force her to smuggle drugs into the prison when visiting her boyfriend. Scott had tried to resist the pressure but security footage had shown James entering Scott's cell moments before he tried to hang himself. Police were following up on some leads and it was highly likely that charges may be laid. For the time being, James had been removed from the unit pending further investigations.

David re-enters the unit whilst I'm on the phone and offers us a half-hearted wave. I hear Meagan groan slightly behind me but try to ignore it. I've never been one to enjoy tension between officers. 12 hours of sitting in a tiny officer's station with added tension is not my idea of a good time. Plus, the crooks pick up on it and try and use it to their advantage.

I hang up and share the news with the other two just as control calls for count. Meagan has already grabbed the muster and asks David to help her as I start preparing movement slips for the gym, education and medical appointments. Fridays can also be notorious for visits but those will be done as they're needed.

It doesn't take long for the unit to be a hive of activity once count is called correct and the day's usual train begins to roll on familiar tracks. Breakfast, gym, education, laundry and early exercise routines all commencing from the get-go. The medical trolley rolls in a short time later and I go and help with the dispensing.

Halfway through, I hear Meagan raising her voice to a crook who's standing in the middle of the unit just grinning at her. He's wearing his hat inside and she's yelling, sounding agitated, trying to get him to remove it. I know that it's nothing more than a test and how she handles it is watched by everyone, not just the prisoner involved. The test isn't so much how she talks to him but more so whether she follows up on his refusal.

"Either take it off or I lock you down," I hear her yell at him and he decides to take it off. The reason hats aren't allowed to be worn inside units is because the cameras have trouble identifying faces in case of an incident. Authorities need to be able to positively identify offenders in case of assaults, vandalism, trafficking or worse.

Once the hat is removed, she turns to sit down, glancing at me briefly. I give her a brief nod and she smiles, acknowledging it. It's the first but probably not the last. Prisoners also have a tendency to get bored so have a wide variety of things to amuse them; everything from card games, gym equipment, books and officer baiting. It is what it is and we just have to deal with it on a case by case basis.

But knowing that Meagan was able to handle her test doesn't lower my nervousness thinking about David's. I know it's coming and whether he knows it or not, they will give him a crack before the day is out. If the codes from the previous day weren't so entertaining for them, they would have tested him then. I look at him as he sits in the station, vacantly staring at the computer screen and hope he manages to handle it.

Once the meds are dispensed and the trolley wheeled out again, I return to the station and check the cell searches for the day. 2 of the 3 seem fine, recognizing the names as being of crooks currently studying a barista's course. It's the third name that raises some butterflies for me. Riley Mason is the unit's only IDS prisoner. Because of a current shortage of accommodation around the prison, the unit that houses IDS prisoners is beyond full, requiring some to be spread out to other places. Riley is in this unit because his brother is also here, but much higher functioning than Riley and acting as a sort of mentor. They share a cell together and can normally be dealt with quite easily.

"Let's go David," I say to my offsider and he looks at me over his shoulder.

"Can't Meagan do it today?" he replies and I shake my head.

"Not this one, sorry." I know that apart from being IDS, Riley Mason also has a flag against his name for inappropriate behaviour around female staff. Emails are sometimes sent out when certain prisoners are to be considered more dangerous if left in certain situations and Riley has a history of sexual misconduct when in the company of females.

David groans but stands to follow me and I lead the way to the cell located on the bottom tier. It's closed and David passes me, walking with attitude, obviously pissed off with having to conduct this particular duty. It doesn't phase me much, my only concern being the welfare and safety of officers and if I can avoid a situation then I will. David on the other hand still hadn't figured it out but I knew time wouldn't be on his side.

When living in a unit, there are certain "unwritten" rules that one should try and abide by. Some of these can be put down to nothing more than common courtesy and following them, even by officers, can sometimes avoid confrontations. One of those is knocking on a door. I'm not saying as an officer you should knock and wait to be invited in. That would be silly and stupid as the crook would simply spend a few minutes hiding their contraband while keeping you waiting. But tapping your key on the door before opening the cell door is a courteous cue that you are about to enter. If the prisoner is in a "delicate position" it gives them a split-second opportunity to call out. We still open the door of course but the warning had been given.

The most common "hang on" we tend to get when wanting access to a cell is the unfortunate crook being in the middle of a toilet stop. Personally, I know I don't want to walk in on someone taking a shit but cracking the door even slightly and seeing them sitting on the can is enough to confirm what they're doing, thereby giving us reason not to enter. It's not like we want to stand there watching him wipe.

Unfortunately, David didn't consider the consequences of ripping open a door that stood closed; not locked but just closed for privacy sake. Without knocking or calling out, he simply pulled the cell door open and began to walk in.

There was a table with 5 seated prisoners, located only a few feet from the said cell and when the cell's occupant began screaming insults at the surprised officer, all 5 crooks turned and began to cheer loudly, pointing at the unfortunate Riley Mason who was lying on his bunk bed with half an arm disappearing into his anus while the other was tugging his dick. He was still trying to remove it as I reached the cell and was yelling insults at David with a face the colour of port wine.

When he finally stood and pulled his trackpants up, I waved at the crooks seated at the table to hush a little. There were more coming around to take a look and I pulled the door slightly shut behind me, despite the putrid stink of shit filling the cell. I was about to call for Riley to jump in the shower and "clean" the offending appendage but it seemed David had other thoughts.

"Leave your pants off, gonna strip you anyway," he grumbled at Riley and before he had a chance to react, instantly realized the error of his ways.

Cells aren't notorious for being huge. Riley wasn't a small prisoner, standing around 6' 1 with a sizeable belly to match. David wasn't small either and so the distance between the two was less than 5 feet, nowhere near enough room to provide enough reaction time if anything was to kick off.

The fist that came flying, was sent with no warning and with the speed of a spooked cat. Still covered with enough shit to paint a mural, it hit David square in the face, sending him backwards into me with the dark smears of Riley's faecal matter wiped across his repulsed expression. The yell of disgusted protest that I felt build in his chest never made it out as I dragged him out of the cell by the scruff of the neck.

"Back," I screamed, pointing a finger at Riley who stood where he had, too stunned by his own success as a grin continued to broaden across his face. He froze in place, that vacant stare watching us as we stepped out into the unit, then disappeared as I slammed the cell door home, locking him inside. The crooks that were still sitting at the table were in gales of laughter as they watched David frantically wipe the shit from his face, one stringy bit dangling from one nostril.

"Hahaha, oh my fucken lord. It's Officer Shit-Lips," one suddenly screams and it sounded like the entire unit erupted into a chorus of cheers, the name instantly catching on. It's a name that will quickly spread around the units and follow the officer wherever he's posted. David is frantically wiping at his face as the deep retching seems to grip him like a vice, his throat gagging in near convulsions.

"Code Alpha, prisoner contained," I call through my radio and control respond by announcing it across the prison. It doesn't take long for help to arrive as David disappears into the staff toilet to attempt to disinfect his face, the retching echoing through the door and out into the unit. As humorous as it may seem to some, there is a real possibility of disease and David will have to subject himself to several tests. I don't know whether any actually made it into his mouth but if it did, then he would need to quarantine himself for up to 3 months from contact with his family. I'm not saying he needs to lock himself in a room but rather cease bodily contact with them by no kissing etc.

Officers begin to lock the unit down and once everyone is back in their cells, remove Riley from his and escort him to the Admissions wing for formal interviews. The police will also be called and Riley will more than likely be transferred to one of the management units. Once he's out of the unit, Meagan heads for the now vacant cell with a bag in hand and proceeds to conduct a cell clearance; itemising items on a list before bagging them, ready to transfer his property into storage.

If Riley *is* transferred to one of the management units, he won't have access to his property until he serves whatever punishment in isolation the supervisor sees fit to impose. That's aside from whatever charges are laid and subsequent sentence from a magistrate. For us, we can only continue with our day. David is sent off to the medical wing to be checked out, not only to remove any lingering turds but to also have his face assessed for injury due to the punch.

To my utmost surprise, he returns to the unit an hour or so later, rejecting the sup's offer to take the rest of the day home. The respect I had for him before the incident just increased 10-fold as I watched him return. He gives me a thumbs up as he enters the station and takes a seat. He begins to chuckle a little and when I turn to look at him speaks just two words.

"Shit-Lips," is all he can manage before breaking out into laughter. It's loud enough for the crooks to hear and to my surprise, no-one responds. I see that he's trying some reverse psychology on the prisoners and I have no doubt it'll work for the most part. It reminds me of a line from Game of Thrones. Tyrion is talking to Jon about being a bastard and Jon is getting all fired up at the name he's being called.

"Never forget what you are and you can wear it like armour," I think is how it goes, or something like it. In other words, accept the name and let it wash over you like water off a duck's back, the insult therefore never hurting you. I think it will work for him. Only time will tell of course but I'm happy he came back to face the horde.

Meagan finished the cell clearance a half hour later and apart from writing a couple of reports, the rest of the day was pretty much a non-event. Good for us, not so for you. But you know from experience that there's always more drama to come, especially in this place.

The afternoon slips by with relative ease and to my surprise, David begins to join in with some of the activities without needing to be asked. By the time we walk out of the gates a few hours later, my opinion of him had turned around completely. I knew that he was posted with myself and Meagan in the same unit tomorrow and am keen to see how he handles the banter which I know is coming.

Although a bit shitty, today was an OK sort of day.

Today I was stationed in the medical wing for a shift, surprised as I thought I was due to work in Thomson West again. Although it can be one of the quieter units, things can get pretty hectic in a heartbeat. I was surprised to see Meagan in the officer's station already and soon after greeting her, saw Thelma coming through the airlock.

"Morning Thelma," I said as she waved at us and then proceeded to introduce her to Meagan. The night-shift officer was just returning from a quick bathroom stop before heading out into the bright morning. We all waved her off then began to conduct a couple of morning checks. Thelma jumped on the emails while Meagan and I prepared for count. I grabbed the muster while she went and retrieved the ligature knife from the top draw.

For those unaware, the ligature knife is required to be carried during a muster in case we find a prisoner hanging from a rope or something similar. Because it is essentially a blade within a prison, it doesn't have a sharpened end, only a blade that wraps back on itself to form a u-shape, preventing it from being used as a stabbing instrument.

There aren't too many prisoners kept in the medical wing and our count only takes a little over 5 minutes. We return to the station with a total of 19 prisoners and I call it in once control calls for numbers. It's not too long before they call it correct and we commence our morning unlock.

Although a normal unit would unlock their entire clientele, the medical unit is quite different, the reason being the prisoner's classifications. This is a mixed unit, meaning we house both mainstream and protection prisoners. Segregation is still required and enforced so only one or the other is let out at any one time.

This morning, it's protection prisoner's turn for an early let-out. Tomorrow it'll be the other way around, just to keep things interesting.

As I make my way around the unit, crooks begin to emerge from their rooms as soon as they hear the click of the unlock, my key snapping each door open with a short rattle. I'm greeted by a number of them as they come out and I respond back, acknowledging each of them.

Once the 11 protections are out and about, I return to the officer's station where Thelma is checking the morning's transfers. There's 1 leaving us and 2 due to arrive from another prison. We have 14 spare beds and 4 empty observation cells and experience tells us that they can all be filled within hours, particularly the obso's.

Obso's are cells that contain cameras, the feeds of which not only run to monitors on our desk but also back to the control room. There are quite a few obso's scattered around the prison and are normally filled with prisoners requiring monitoring, either on suicide watch or medical watch. The obso's in this unit are some of the most active due to it's location and thus have a very high turnover of occupants. It's rare to find them all empty, like today.

"James, your transferring out today. You want to go and start packing?" Thelma calls to a prisoner who's walking past us. He nods and heads back to his cell, an extra bounce in his hobble, clearly happy to be leaving.

One of the nurses passes us, waving as he heads around the cells to conduct his trap checks. This entails dropping the trap, poking his head in and taking a visual check of the occupants. These types of checks are held every 2 hours, throughout the 24-hour period, night and day. I return his wave and then ask Thelma to print off the incoming list, which gives us the names, details and classification of the new crooks. I check and see that there's one of each, making it easy to place them into the unit.

We have different sized cells in here, most being 4-outers. These contain 4 beds and one bathroom for them to share, much like a normal hospital room, containing shower, sink and toilet. Hanging down from the ceiling between the facing beds are televisions which are housed in a safety box. Although each bed has their own TV, all 4 are linked to ensure the sound is the same. Cell occupants have to agree on what to watch as one remote (held in the officer's station) controls the entire unit. Want to change channel? Buzz the officer and they'll bring it to you.

"Help please?" is suddenly called and I look up to see the nurse standing by one of the locked cells. He's waving for us and I rush to him, Meagan following close behind, calling for the unit to be locked down. Thelma calls the code mike and starts locking them in from the other end, while I peek in through the trap to ensure there's no threat. "He's not responding," the nurse says as I unlock the door and he rushes past me as I hear several other nursing staff heading towards us.

The unit is locked down in under 2 minutes as the nurses begin working on the unresponsive prisoner. He's old and frail looking, skinny to the point of emaciation. It may surprise you to learn that a medical code is called, despite us being in the medical wing, but this is so several things happen. The staff that are on response immediately attend the unit, as well as the duty supervisor. Control puts the code protocol in place which means all non-essential radio traffic ceases. This process makes it easier and more efficient when needing to call for ambulances and extra services and staff.

Nursing staff request an ambulance to be called and the duty supervisor requests one from control who'll make the call and organise its escort to the unit once it arrives. Being a prison, the ambulance still needs to enter via the same access point as any other traffic but isn't subjected to internal searches.

The nurses continue working on the prisoner as the supervisor stands the code down, excusing the extra staff from the unit who immediately leave, leaving Thelma, Meagan and myself to stand guard. The supervisor leaves to organise an officer to accompany the ambulance back to the hospital, as every prisoner leaving a prison must have either one or two officers present to watch them at all times, depending on their rating.

This particular prisoner is a Class-4 rating, the lowest threat possible, requiring a single unarmed escort. If he was a Class-1, then he'd have 4 fully armed officers as well as be completely shackled with cuffs and leg-irons.

Thelma returns to the station to type up the report for calling the code while Meagan and I remain just outside the door of the cell. This particular prisoner is in a single one so thankfully, we don't have other roommates to consider. With the unit locked up for the duration of the episode, it makes it a lot easier for us to deal with the multitude of people coming and going from the unit.

The ambulance arrives almost 15 minutes after the call is made. They arrive with their stretcher, perform a brief check of the patient, then have a team lift him onto it so he can be transferred aboard. An officer carrying a folder and personal bag arrives and escorts the fanfare back to the ambulance, leaving us to return to the usual daily routine.

Once we confirm the ambulance has left the building, I re-unlock the unit to a few cheers, the day back on its usual track. It's not long before the crooks are shuffling around the corridors, some either simply pacing this way and that and others running their errands which can entail changing books by the bookshelf or heading out into the exercise yard, the day a sunny one.

Us officers take care of our duties with Thelma showing Meagan how to add new prisoners onto the muster and finding them a bed in the cell allocation spreadsheet. She's a quick learner and when Thelma offers Meagan the computer to finish the second one on her own, does so with very little guidance. It's a process she will undertake on an almost daily basis and it won't take long to become second nature.

With very little else happening, the next stop on our tour of duty is lunchtime muster, a brief moment of prisoner interaction that is over within a few minutes. Although the unit is run like a hospital wing, it is still technically a prison, a place where both worlds tend to live in relative harmony. The nurses conduct their duties and responsibilities while we take care of ours. Sometimes clashes can occur between the nurses and us, especially when a new staff member commences their duties, inexperience normally to blame.

A new nurse began her first shift just after 10 o'clock and just as control calls for all movement to cease, approaches Meagan to unlock one of the cells to conduct a check. I hear Meagan explain that it's muster but her response is one that doesn't sit well with me.

"I wasn't asking, sweetheart," she said with a thick accent. I looked up to see colour flush the young officer's cheeks, clearly taken by surprise.

"I'm sorry, I can't. Not until after count," Meagan replied, trying her best to sound apologetic but it seemed like this nurse just thought herself a little better than the prison officer.

"Is there a problem?" Thelma asks from behind me and I see the nurse actually roll her eyes.

"Oh look, here comes your back-up," she mutters, eyeing Thelma.

"Excuse me? Did you just roll your eyes at me?" Thelma asks now on her feet. Although standing a little scrape above the 5-foot mark, she has a big set of lungs and the balls to use them. What the nurse doesn't realise is that Thelma has been mixing it in maximum security for over a decade and doesn't shy away from conflict, although not one to go looking for it. What does set her off is when new officers are taken advantage of.

As I watch Thelma home in on the nurse, I see the attitude slowly drain from her face as the much shorter officer closes in.

"There's no movement once the control room calls it. If you have an issue with that, feel free to take it up with the sup. Extension 794 in case you need the number." Thelma locks on to the nurse's eyes, staring her down until she finally shakes her head and turns away. And then loud enough for the nurse to hear, Thelma adds a little fuel to the fire by speaking to Meagan.

"Don't let the inexperienced try and dictate to you, sweetheart. Takes time for them to realise where they're at." The nurse doesn't turn around, instead making a beeline for another nurse standing in their windowed office. They both begin to whisper to each other, looking like a couple of high-schoolers, glancing sideways at us every so often.

I remember back when I first began, I too had a run in with a nurse. She ended up phoning the sup who rightly put her in her place, explaining that we weren't there to make life difficult for the medical staff, instead trying to keep them safe. But unfortunately, some people struggle with a lack of perceived authority and that particular nurse never spoke to me again, eventually transferring out of the prison a couple of years later.

Count is called correct a short time after we call our number in and the same nurse approaches me to accompany her to her previous destination. She speaks the bare minimum to me and I don't get a thank you when I close the cell door upon her completion. I'm not too fussed, having more serious matters to manage.

Apart from a code mike in Tambo West, there's no other excitement to speak of and when we head out a short time after lockdown, wish each other a good night. Today was a good day.

I pass Thelma on my way in and she tells me that the prisoner from the previous morning had passed away just as he arrived at the hospital. He was 82-years old and convicted for "tampering" with his neighbour's daughter. I wish her a good day and continue on to my shift in the Visit's Centre.

There are already 3 officers seated in the back and after greeting each of them, make my way through to the front where I'm welcomed by 2 more. A third joins us a few minutes later, an old guy called Joseph McDonald. Joseph has been an active correctional officer for over 30 years and the grin on his face tells me that there's more than just the sunshine cheering him up.

"You all good, Joe?" I ask as he throws his bag in one of the cupboards that line the inside of the station.

"You haven't heard?" Tom Grady said from behind me and I turn to shake hands with him.

"Heard what?" I ask, confused.

"Well, let's just say the cake in the fridge isn't for his birthday," Chris Upton chirps over his shoulder.

"Joe?" I ask, looking at the old man, his cheeks flushing a little.

"It's my last day today," he said, the happiness sounding more like relief as he speaks.

"Holy shit, man. That's awesome." I shake hands with him, congratulating him with a hearty slap on the back. He coughs comically and Chris tells me to take it easy, otherwise the old man might fall over before his final holidays even begin.

The average life-span of an active officer is less than 3 years, so seeing one make it past 30 and into retirement earns pretty high praise in my book. By lifespan, I don't mean actually alive; I'm referring to their lifespan as an active officer before quitting or being asked to leave.

"And just to make it even more fun," Chris said from his seat at the computer, holding up a piece of paper he'd just printed off. "Here's today's list, people." Tom grabs it from his fingers and immediately chuckles into his hand, holding the page up for all to see.

It's blank, the columns devoid of their usual names and times.

"What?" I ask, unsure of the meaning.

"It's a legal day," Chris said, saying it more like a question as if speaking to a child. I nod, finally understanding. Legal days are when prisoner's legal councils can visit with them. It's no different than normal other than the fact there can be a lot more allowed, due to the rest of the centre being empty. It'll still be a fairly active day, but nowhere near as busy as when we have a list of keen family and friends wanting to see their loved ones.

Lawyers have never needed to make an appointment, able to simply turn up. Once they are comfortably seated in the centre, we contact the unit to send the specific prisoner up for their visit. The sessions aren't really timed either, giving their legal counsel a relatively stress-free visit. But prisoners in prison are already under stress, often strained by not only the environment, but also by the constant fear of a pending court case. When they meet with their legal representative, crooks only really want to hear one thing; when they'll get out.

There are of course those that know they won't be getting out anytime soon. Those that have been in and out of prison know the way things work, understanding that sometimes they need to serve the time for the crime they committed.

Our phone rings and Chris answers it, looking at me as he's talking. Just as he thanks the caller, he flashes me a thumbs up and I take the cue to go and collect whoever is waiting at the front door, ready to be escorted to the centre.

When I open the reception airlock, I see 2 men and a woman, all dressed in their finest suits and carrying leather folders. I greet them and they follow me back to Visits, none bothering to talk to the lonely officer. Once back, they head to the desk and speak to Tom who collects the names of the lucky prisoners, then assigns each lawyer to a private visit's room, which are located across two of the centre's walls. Chris phones the appropriate units and our day begins.

The visits proceed with relative ease, prisoners coming and going throughout the morning, the 9 rooms almost filling completely at one point. We hear yelling a few times but when we approach the windowed doors, are waved away by the visitors like flies being shooed.

It's not until we find one poor soul who's practically pinned to a wall that we intervene. This particular prisoner is facing a murder charge and has been extremely vocal about his innocence. When we hear the voices begin to rise, 3 of us hurry to the door, the yells rising to almost fever pitch by the time we reach it. The unfortunate lawyer, a middle-aged man who looks to struggle in a strong wind, is standing with his back to one wall. The prisoner had picked up a chair and pushed the legs against the man, pinning him like mouse in a trap.

We push through the door and grab the crook, dragging him from the room and to the back of the centre while he's continuing to abuse and threaten his rep.

"Get me the fuck outa here or I'll send someone after your kids. Fucken do it," he screams, struggling against us as his pale-faced lawyer stays standing there with a panicked grin on his face.

Once we've isolated the crook in the back with the three of the officers there, we return back to the room where the man is still standing, visibly shaking from his experience.

"Well that was rude," is all he says to no one in particular before finally packing up and waiting for his escort back to the front. He doesn't speak until we reach the final airlock where he offers me a whispered thank you before heading inside, clearly relieved to be leaving.

Lunchtime muster comes and is finished without a hiccup as we begin our afternoon stretch. It gets quite hectic at one point when we have 8 legal reps turn up at once but all the visits finish in record time and before it hits 3 o'clock, our unit is down to dribs and drabs as 1's and 2's come and go. Some visits are nothing more than a minute as the prisoner is simply required to sign some form the lawyer wishes to lodge with whichever court is required and these are simply walk in and walk out affairs.

The only incident that occurs during the afternoon run is one lawyer, a young guy feeling especially important, getting himself a blood lip courtesy of a swift backhander from his chosen crook. Their visit seemed to have gone without a hitch, both emerging from the room with smiles less than 10 minutes after entering. The prisoner had asked the lawyer when he would get his mother's signature as he walked out behind the rep. The man had replied with a carefree tone that didn't sit well with the crook, a large islander with a short fuse.

"When I get around to it," he'd said. The crook made an "oi" sound and when the unsuspecting guy turned to look at his client, felt nothing more than his head snap to the left as a backhanded slap struck him so fast, it was over before anyone realised what had happened. We were on our feet in a second but the prisoner was already standing aside with his hands held out in front of him, ready and waiting for the cuffs. The lawyer stood with a shocked expression on his face, a sliver of blood running down the side of his chin, as little droplets began to adorn his silver suit like tiny red beads.

Chris was the first to reach them, cuffing the crook who was grinning at the surprised expression on his lawyer's face while Tom called the code Alpha.

"Don't speak to me like that, Bro," he simply said before being led away. The man looked at us dumbfounded, trying to make sense of what just happened. Officers begin to enter but with the prisoner already cuffed and fully compliant, there's very little for them to do.

It'll mean an extra assault charge for the crook, already facing two for a bar fight. He's a regular visitor to our establishment and is what you'd call an "easy-timer", a prisoner who sees prison as nothing more than a bit of rest and relaxation.

We are all required to write reports which takes a good half hour, given the lack of computers to go around. But once we finish, the phone calls from the front had completely ceased, our slapped visitor the final one for the day.

With a half hour to go before the end of our shift, one of the tables is slowly filled with all manner of food, snacks, cakes and sandwiches. Cups and bottles of juice are also added and before long, like ants finding a dropped ice-cream cone, officers begin to pile in for the free feed, courtesy of our retiree.

Beginning his prison career back in 1986, Joe had worked at 3 prisons in total, ours being his longest and final one with 19 years. During his time in service, he'd witnessed several riots, numerous stabbings and countless assaults. He'd seen colleagues attacked, injured, spat at and targets for faecal missiles. But Joe had made it without ever suffering an attack himself. He was an honest officer who understood what "duty of care without prejudice" really meant and always followed it, as far as I know.

Numerous officers come and pay tribute to him, many of them shaking his hand for the final time, including me. They tell war stories throughout the rest of the afternoon, continuing as I head out with Chris and Tom, leaving Joe to enjoy the rest of his final shift as an officer.

Today was an awesome day.

After having such a great day yesterday, I jump at the chance to work in the visit's centre again when offered it. I know that both Chris and Tom will be there and am surprised to see Kon sitting out the back as I walk through the airlock. We shake hands and I ask him about the weekend he'd just had. He told me the previous week that it was his 25th wedding anniversary on the Saturday and had arranged to take his wife away for the night. The smile on his face told me more than his words and I clapped him on the back, congratulating him on such an amazing milestone.

Scott Jones suddenly comes through the far door and I shake with him as a third officer arrives through the airlock. The face is unfamiliar to me and when I introduce myself, find his name to be Lee Harrison, a young lad from the recent graduates.

"Leave you to it, boys," I said and head towards the front where a full crew is already waiting for the first phone call. I see that Daryl Foster is the escorting officer today, leaving me to take a seat by the phone, officially running the station. By having one officer take care of phone calls, seat and room allocations and notifying units of visitor arrivals, leaves the rest of the crew to focus on the visits taking place, monitoring the tables and rooms either directly or via the monitors on our desk.

It doesn't take long for the first phone call to come through and I give Daryl the thumbs up to head to the front and collect the first round of visitors. Chris turns the monitors on while Tom continues to read his emails. Within a few minutes, the centre is alive with activity as a number of small children begin to tear the play area apart as the grown-ups patiently await the prisoner's arrival.

Once I have the names ticked off my list, I proceed to contact the units, advising the names required to attend. It doesn't take long for the majority to arrive, keen to meet with their loved ones. It's a cycle that will continue throughout the day, only pausing once while changing from mainstream to protection.

The phone rings and when I answer, am told that a visitor for Prisoner Ascot has tested positive for cocaine and has accepted a box visit. Random visitors are given a drug swab upon entering the prison and if traces of drugs are found, have to submit to a strip search. They can refuse but are then subject to a 12-month ban on attending the prison. If they do submit to a strip search and pass, are then offered a box visit. If drugs *are* found upon their person, they are confiscated and both the drugs and visitor handed to police.

This particular visitor had submitted to a strip search and passed and has also accepted the box visit as a final option. I know from experience that the crew in the back are the ones tasked with advising the prisoner in the change of plans, the notification being one of the most common times for things to get volatile.

But when the prisoner turns up, he accepts the change with very little fuss, knowing that the onus is on the visitor. But his calm demeanour doesn't last long as he challenges his girlfriend the instant the door is shut.

"Why the fuck you taking? You said no more," he's heard to scream through the glass. Chris does a walk-past to ensure the room isn't being damaged and stays within close proximity. The voices soon calm and the visit continues without incident, Chris eventually returning to his post.

When he returns 40 minutes later to give the couple their 10-minute warning, he finds the woman standing with her top lifted and her hand down the front of her pants while the prisoner is sitting back in his chair and masturbating his exposed dick. Both seem to be having a wonderful time and aren't too pleased when

Chris begins hammering on the door. But timing wasn't in his favour, the crook shooting just as Chris bangs on the door for the second time. The woman flashed him a grin of accomplishment while the prisoner puts his dick away, waving at the officer. In the adjoining cubicle, a prisoner continues his box visit with his wife and 2 small children.

Chris heads for the bathroom and grabs a handful of paper towel, returning to the room and handing it to the crook to clean. He does so as his girlfriend watches on, giggling as her man is made to wipe his cum off the walls and floor. There will be a six-month ban imposed on the girlfriend which neither seem too fussed about and we find out why later when the prisoner's wife turns up with their 3 children to visit with him.

You've already read plenty of stories from the visit's centre and I won't bore you with more non-eventful happenings. The afternoon flies along as we process prisoners and visitors both in and out, until the last finally leaves just before 5. There's very little to do once the centre is empty and I'm happy to end another shift as we walk out mere moments later. Although the day is extremely unpredictable in the centre, it's still one of my favourite places to work.

Today was a great day.

Monday, November 12

Returning after a 4-day weekend is never easy but I would never say no to one. The days away give me plenty of quality writing time and I often surprise myself with how many pages I get through by the time I return to work.

Today I'm rostered in Yarra North, happy to be working with Meagan and Kon. From the moment I see her step through the airlock, I can tell that Meagan's confidence has increased dramatically. It's a positive sign and I greet her as she enters the station.

"How's work been?" I ask and she explains her previous day to me, an overtime shift in Murray North where she was introduced to the work ethics of one Tony Malone. I nod my understanding, having experienced his ethics personally on many occasions.

Kon arrives halfway through the story and when he hears some of its contents, mouths the name "Tony" at me questioningly. I nod a second time, Kon firing up the computer while brandishing an understanding grin on his face. Meagan finishes her war story and breathes a sigh of relief.

"Glad to get that off my chest," she said, putting her bag away.

"No transfers for us," Kon says, continuing to brows his emails. It's one less thing for us to take care off. Transfers in or out create a wake of extra duties, mostly concerning cell allocations. If a prisoner transfers out and happens to vacate a single cell then the flow-on effect it leaves can lead to conflict and headaches from prisoners and staff alike. The struggle for a single cell is never ending.

As I'm about to grab the muster board, Meagan beats me to it, leading the way towards the first door. I drop each trap, greeting those prisoners that are awake, while rousing those that aren't, calling out the numbers as we proceed around the unit until we have our final tally.

Meagan adds her numbers while I check my emails, checking gym times, education and medical appointments. These can often change throughout the day but it gives us somewhere to start. Being a protection unit, all our prisoners are escorted wherever they need to go and just as Meagan calls in her number to control, our fourth officer arrives into the unit. It's David, the officer with the very unfortunate nickname that still seems to be sticking just as its namesake.

"Hey," I call as he enters the station. He offers handshakes all 'round and then asks if we have any moves yet.

"After unlock. There'll be a few moves to begin with," I said, showing him the computer screen. He peers at it, slowly nodding through the names.

Count is called correct moments later and Megan and I head back out to release the horde into the day. Several make a beeline for the station to ask a question I already know is coming. Kon is there to greet them and as I see him shaking his head from side to side, know what the curious few were wanting to know; whether there were any transfers out. The look of displeasure on each of their faces is enough to tell me just how disappointed they are. I couldn't imagine what it would be like to have to live with one of these inmates 24/7, listening to every bodily function and enduring every aroma throughout each day and night.

David has his first group, 17 methadones, ready to rock 'n roll a minute later and they head out through the airlock with animated excitement. They return within 20 minutes, a little ahead of the med-trolley that's slowly making its own rounds. As Kon calls for medications over the PA system, a line begins to form in front of the dispensing window. Nearly the entire unit is lined up, the queue almost as long as the length of the bottom tier. As each prisoner reaches the front, they flash their ID card, recite their prison number and then patiently wait for their cup of goodies, some filled more than others.

27 pills are the most I've ever seen in one cup, the prisoner almost eating a meal of pills. 27. They half-filled a drinking cup and looked full of jelly beans, the prisoner simply drinking them down in 3 large swallows, paid for by the taxes from you and I.

It's almost 30 minutes before the final pills are dispensed, Kon giving the unit a final call as the last of the prisoners head back to their cells. There's a hive of activity outside in the exercise yard with several prisoners giving the washing machines a workout.

It's just normal day to day stuff as the morning's activities play out as they do most days. David returns, sometimes with crooks and sometimes without, each time leaving within minutes to deliver a new prisoner to some exciting destination. While I print off the list of random cell searches, Meagan is busy sorting out an issue with bedding. 3 new arrivals from the previous day had been locked up without any bedding, spending a fairly fresh night sleeping fully clothed.

There's a sudden commotion from one of the upper-tier cells and when Kon and I approach, are confronted with a prisoner lying face down on the floor, his face dripping blood. As he slowly turns to look up at us, I can see 2 teeth lying on the floor beneath him.

"Bradley, what the hell man?" Kon asks, squatting down to help the crook up. He's a young guy, in for suspected rape and murder and our initial thoughts are that he's been attacked in his cell.

"Fell off my fucken bed," he tries to tell us. It's a 2-outer and Bradley occupies the top bunk. "Was trying to change the channel," he continues, pointing at the TV sitting on the desk which sat on the opposite wall. I call a code Mike and wait for the medics to arrive while Kon returns to the station to call control. They'll rewind the camera footage and see if anyone entered or exited the cell in the previous hour or so.

By the time the nurses leave with an injured prisoner, control calls Kon to confirm that no one had entered or exited his cell at all. From what we could gather, he'd tried to lean across the 4-foot gap between bed and TV and lost his grip, tumbling to the floor face first and knocking out two of his teeth plus cutting his lip. Both Kon and I write up our reports and email them to the sup. By the time lunchtime count is called correct, we begin the afternoon side of things with a clean slate.

As the hours tick by, the only person really doing anything is David and before I have a chance to swap with him, find Meagan already ahead of me as she calls for a couple of names to escort to the medical unit for their appointments. She leaves the airlock with the prisoners in tow as David grabs a seat in the station, heartily chomping down on a block of chocolate.

The prisoners begin to settle into the afternoon with various activities on offer around the unit. There's the usual pool game, table tennis play-offs, card games and chess tournaments. The gym also attracts a few partakers and out in the exercise yard, several prisoners are perfectly happy just pacing back and forth in the sunshine.

The three of us enjoy the quiet time, mixing it up with war stories, jokes and bits of gossip heard around the traps. The gossip consists mainly of who is seeing who and who's been walked out over allegations. The latter is normally for either sleeping on the job or trying to smuggle cigarettes into the prison, a sad reality of the environment we work in. But every now and then, a juicy piece of gossip will do the rounds, told with deep enthusiasm by the sharer of said news. David tells us that he heard that one of the women had been walked off for being caught in a crook's cell after hours.

The unfortunate truth is that it actually happens a lot more than people realise, the average of two females being sacked each and every year. But when David tells me the name of the latest discovery, I'm shocked beyond belief, not because of the act but rather who the person is. Her name is Gail Humphries and it's a real shock to me because the lady had been an officer for as long as me, having been on the same intake course together. She was always so anti-crook, often going out of her way to ensure that any breach of rules was dealt with swiftly and harshly. She was also married with 3 children, all teenagers.

The prisoner she supposedly visited, was in for a string of robbery and drug offences, by no means a stranger to the inside. His prisoner number was of someone first into the system last century, when he was still in his very late teens. I was floored beyond belief.

"Wow, you just never know," was all I could manage.

"Fuck off, cunt," suddenly came from one of the tables near the front. A game of poker had been slowly proceeding and it looked to have just blown up over a difference of opinions.

"Guys," Kon called out.

"Boss, we both got 2 8's. Who wins? I say it's a tie and we replay the hand," one of the crooks calls out.

"Your next highest card is played," Kon replies and one of the other crooks begins to cheer, holding up the ace of spades for all to see. The first crook throws his cards down in disgust but remains at the table, not wanting to be labelled a sore loser.

The afternoon continues with very little excitement, the unit cruising through the final med trolley, dinner and final muster with relative ease. Once the unit is locked down and our prisoners are all tucked in, we head out into the fading light, happy that another one is done and dusted.

Today was a pretty good day.

I'm back in Yarra North again and to my surprise, see Kon already in the station when I enter. But his expression isn't one of happiness, a frown of anger on his face.

"Hey, everything OK?" I ask as I near him. He hesitates for a moment then turns to me.

"I found a joint in Nick's room last night," he said, almost whispering. Nick is Kon's 9-year old son.

"Oh man, I'm sorry." Kon hesitates again, then slowly nods.

"Dope," he says awkwardly, the heaviness of his voice now so low that I strain to hear the rest of his words. "Told me he'd only tried it a couple of times, but." He paused, gazing at me with a look I knew to mean I already knew the answer. "My kid's a drug addict, Simon. He's just 9-years old and a junkie," he said now losing control of his emotions as Thelma came through the airlock. Kon rose and went to the staff toilet, giving Thelma a brief wave as he passed her.

"What's wrong with him?" she asked but I just shook my head.

"That he'll have to tell you himself."

"Oh, that bad, huh?" she asks and I nod at her.

"Yeah, that bad."

Kon emerges from the bathroom just as Thelma and I finish our count. She tallies up the number then calls it in as Kon returns with 3 cups of coffee, holding one out to each of us. When we sit and wait for count to called correct, Kon shares his news with Thelma who is just as shocked as I was. We sip our drinks as we discuss the options open to Kon, a parent who's always been there for his children.

Thelma is just as stunned, more-so by the young age of the child in question. Her advice is to visit with his school and find out who he's getting it from. I'm totally floored, having young children myself. It appears there's no hiding from the drug epidemic that seems to be gripping the world.

Count is called correct just as I finish my coffee and follow Thelma out to help with the unlock. It's not long before the familiar shuffle of feet and excited voices fill the air as freshly unlocked crooks jostle for positions at the toasters, washing machines and officer's station.

"Anyone leaving?" asks one.

"Gym today, Boss?" asks another.

"Where's my name on the single cell list?" asks another. Just as Kon pulls up the list of transfers, Chris Upton comes through the airlock, our escorting officer for the day. The prisoners keen for their morning methadone dose instantly surround him like flies around a discarded bone. Once the final call is made and no one else appears to want to join the field trip, he leads the pack out of the unit, leaving us to deal with the crowd before us.

"Turner, Lazenby. Go pack your things, lads. You're out of here," Kon tells the crowd. There's an instant holler of voices as the group realise both transfers occupy single cells, opening up 2 vacant possibilities. Thelma chuckles a little as the voices gain definite excitement; the all important single-cell list finally produced.

"And the winners are," Thelma begins, glancing over the group who instantly hush. She pauses for dramatic effect, locking eyes with each of her audience in turn.

"Come on, Miss," one finally says, breaking the silence of the rest. Thelma holds her hand up for silence and only once she gets it, reveals the next 2 names on the list.

"Gavin Maher and Richard Huggett." There's a split second of hushed silence as the names appear to be considered and then the wild commotion restarts as cries of disagreement and objection begin.

"But I was here before Gavin. How come he's ahead of me?" one starts but they all know Thelma well enough. The names stick and the list is swiftly returned to its hiding spot in the bottom drawer.

The excited winners of the single cells hurry back to their homes and begin to pack, an entourage of onlookers following them, hoping for any handouts that may ensue during the moving period. Gavin is the first to emerge from his second-tier cell, slowly descending the stairs while carrying a single bag of possessions. He stands beside the door of his new cell whilst its current occupant finishes his own cleanout.

It's not long before both of the transfers are waiting patiently by the airlock, quietly awaiting Chris's return. When he does, he doesn't bother coming inside, simply waving for the crooks to come out to him. He shoots me a wave to confirm the transfer and continues about his duty while I head to the computer for the day's cell searches.

One of the cells to be searched turns out to be offline due to a leaking toilet, saving us a bit of time. The second cell is for a lifer on the bottom tier who's been in the unit for close to 10 years, easily the longest serving in Yarra North. To my surprise, the third cell is one that had only just been vacated, now occupied by Gavin Maher. I show the list to Kon and he chuckles a little at the last cell on the list.

"Is what it is, I guess," he says and he follows me as we head straight to Gavin's new home.

"Guess what?" I say as I knock on the open door, watching as the crook is placing some t-shirts on a shelf.

"Huh?" he mumbles, turning to me.

"You're up for a search, Gavin."

"What? Are you serious, Boss?'

"Sure am. Just leave your stuff, man. Easier for everybody." He agrees and although not the start he was hoping for, reluctantly strips for us and once given the all clear, exits the cell, leaving Kon and I to go fishing.

We weren't really expecting to find anything, and we almost didn't, but just as we were about to leave, I dropped to the floor and peeked up under a lip of metal under the bunk of the cell. To my surprise, there was something sticky-taped there, wrapped in paper for protection. As I reach up and pull it free, I can already feel what the find is and once I'm back on my feet and peel back the top layer, confirm my suspicions.

There is a wad of about a dozen tailor-made cigarettes, all held together by a sheet of paper towelling, then carefully sticky-taped together.

"Good find," Kon says as I hold the durries up to him. He opens the door and beckons for Gavin to join us. As soon as he enters and sees what I'm holding, his face changes instantly, holding both hands up before him.

"Whatever that is, it's not mine. Fuck man, I just got here."

"But it could have been the first thing you did," I said, holding the package on the palm of my hand.

"A-ah, nope, no way. I'll go back to my old cell if I have to. That ain't mine, Boss." I look at Kon and he shrugs his shoulders, his gesture confirming my thoughts. There's no proof either way.

"Alright, Gavin. Leave it with us," I said, walking out and back to the station.

"Probably Greg Turner's stash," Kon said as we get back and I call the Admissions staff to see whether he's still there. They tell me he is and I phone the sup to tell him of the find. He agrees to question Turner and will call me with the outcome.

When the sup calls back less than an hour later, I'm surprised to learn that Turner had owned up to the package. The sup had simply told him that Gavin would be charged with the stash. Turner knew he was transferring out and although the sup could have phoned his offence through to his next jail, said he wouldn't once Turner accepted responsibility without needing to be coerced. I let Gavin know once I hung up the phone and was glad to put the matter to rest.

And apart from a brief code mike early in the afternoon, there is little else to share. The code mike was for a swollen ankle which we saw happen right in front of us when a crook tripped down the last couple of stairs leading from the top tier. He hit the deck quite hard, his ankle having rolled quite painfully.

Some days, it's just not worth going on and on about meaningless routine which is exactly what the rest of the day was like.

Today was a great day.

Saturday, November 17

First night shifts are always the hardest on the body, especially when you have a cold. That's me tonight. Stupid cold and 12 hours stuck in Murray South. It's not a bad unit really, but no unit is great when you'd rather be in bed relaxing. But there's little I can do about that as I slowly make my way to the unit.

The day staff are tying up loose ends and already conducting final trap musters as I enter the unit, greeted by Vicky Temple who is manning the book.

"Oh boy are you lucky," she told me as soon as I enter the station.

"Huh?" I reply, clueless.

"Toby Manning has just been transferred to Murray North. Little prick bronzed up in 44. It's offline till a cleaning billet fixes it." I instantly realized that the faint fragrance that greeted me the second I stepped inside was shit.

"Oh my God, thank fuck for that," I said, totally agreeing with my offsider.

"First one?" she asked as I sat down, watching the others continue their count.

"Yeah, first of 3. Ugh." The others soon join us and as Robert tally's up the numbers, the rest begin to pack their stuff, readying themselves to sign off for another shift. "Any excitement today?" I ask and most shake their heads.

"Nah, not even a single code. So quiet on the radio." Weekends sometimes feel exactly like they should, even in prison.

It takes the day crew less than 10 seconds to vacate the building once control calls count correct. Their overly-loud conversation fades from my ears as they exit the airlock, a couple of them shooting me a final wave as they disappear from view.

I stand by the station for a few seconds and take in the sounds of the unit. Most of the lights have been turned off and the few that remain lit, struggle to contain the shadows in the corners. Less light reaches the upper tier and there are several patches of darkness in between the few overhead lights that are still lit up. Several TVs are on and I can make out a number of different programs, one being an American comedy, the laughter track unmissable. It's probably Big Bang or something similar, the viewing crook occasionally laughing at whatever funny line had just been delivered.

A toilet flushes near me, somewhere overhead, the trickling of the water sounding crystal clear amongst the other sounds. There's a cough further along and somewhere near the other end, someone is singing along to "Radio Ga Ga".

I head over to the store room and begin my only duty for the night, other than to keep an eye on the unit itself. It's to restock the supply cupboards inside the station. There are certain items that prisoners are entitled to on a daily basis and these are kept close at hand so as to reduce travel time. Tubes of toothpaste, replacement tooth brushes, sponges, detergent, toilet paper and garbage bags are just to name a few. Each item has an allocated shelf in one of the four cupboards and I restock them to acceptable levels to ensure they meet the next day's demand.

Once I finish restocking, I turn my attention to the staff TV, setting it up and scanning the channels for something suitable. An old episode of MacGyver briefly grabs my attention, but it doesn't hold it for long, the remote working overtime to find something more interesting. My finger suddenly freezes in mid-air as Darth Vader's helmet fills my screen and I instantly know I'm set, a Star Wars marathon just the ticket to help me stay awake.

There's a brief moment of excitement when a crook buzzes me at around 2am, but the emergency he needs solved is resolved with the handing over of a toilet roll, a disaster averted in the blink of an eye.

To stay awake in the small hours of the morning, I turn to my writing, punching out pages at a pretty decent rate. There's a second buzz up when a prisoner asks for a piece of fruit at around 5. He's a diabetic and feels his blood sugar-level crashing. I manage to scrounge him up an apple and an orange and he thanks me when I pass them through his trap.

Other than that, its's a pretty bland night shift that was made a little more enjoyable courtesy of the force. Once a couple of day staff arrive, I bid them farewell, knowing that I will return before they finish their shift.

It was a great night.

The second of my nights in Murray South and Vicky greets me again as I come stumbling through the airlock. I say stumbling because I'm walking like a man on the tail-end of a 12-hour shift cutting trees with an axe. My nose is leaking like a prison tap, my back feels like there's a screwdriver lost in it somewhere and my whole body feels like it's giving me the finger.

"You look like shit," Vicky snorts as I drop into a chair next to her.

"Oh yeah, laugh it up, lady." She takes my advice, practically splitting her sides at my expense. When I embed a tissue into my nostril and leave it hanging there while sighing, she laughs even harder.

The others soon join in and I'm ready to walk out with them, given the chance.

"Anything new?" I ask and she shakes her head; a very good sign for me. If the day was fairly quiet then hopefully the night would follow suit and I could be left to my own devices again.

It doesn't take long for the Deja vu to return as count is called correct and the group of happy campers exit through the airlock, sending me a final wave as they round the corner.

The buzzer goes off almost immediately and when I ask what the issue is, am greeted with loud groaning, sounding like a cow with a broken leg. Once I'm able to ascertain the issue, a toothache, I phone the sup to OK an after-hours medical move. I don't really want to call a code and the sup agrees, asking me to contact the nurses. Unfortunately, they don't want to attend the unit, so I call for a couple of staff to conduct a move, taking the crook to the medical wing for some pain relief.

The prisoner is back in his cell with 20 minutes, happy to have swallowed a couple of tablets. I thank the three staff that turned up for the move and they leave the unit giggling at my unfortunate red nose and croaky voice. We part company with the flash of a finger and the words "fuck you" mouthed through the window.

Once the unit is settled again, I finish restocking the supplies then flick on the TV and begin searching for something worthwhile. It's another good night for a TV marathon as I spot Indiana Jones playing on one of the movie channels, the first of the planned 3. It suits me fine, not in the mood for writing due to my diseased head.

I struggle through the wee hours of the morning by pacing around the unit, walking with a slow and steady pace. Although my keys jingle a little, the crooks don't seem to mind as I circumvent the unit several dozen times. The intercom goes off a little after 5 and it's the crook with the tooth problem. I try and get the nurse to attend the unit and this time he accepts, the other option being me calling a code.

I call for an escort and have two volunteers within seconds, both heading to the medical unit to pick up the nurse. Things run so much smoother when people are a bit more forthcoming and I thank the nurse once the crook has been dosed. He returns my handshake and even hangs around for a few minutes to talk a bit of shit but due to the escorting staff having other duties, cut short our conversation.

I don't hang around very long once the day staff arrive a couple of hours later and breathe a sigh of relief as my head hits the pillow a short time later.

When it comes to nightshift, it was an OK sort of night.

Monday, November 19

With 2 shifts down, I push through and arrive for my last night shift a little early, catching up with a couple of officers who are heading the other way. There's a bit of gossip regarding an officer caught handing a prisoner a bag containing white powder, the idiot passing the drugs over right in front of a camera. He was walked off the site pending an investigation and will most likely be charged by police.

It's great to catch up, but when I hear the 15-minute warning till lockdown, head for my unit. I find Chris manning the station while the others are already locking the unit down by conducting their trap muster. It's not long before the usual sequence of events is finished and I'm left to my own devices for another 12 hours.

My cold seems to be easing its hold on me and I breathe a lot easier as I restock the cupboards and answering a couple of intercom calls for toilet paper. The TV is set up shortly after but tonight I find that my urge to write is back with a real hunger, words and phrases circling my brain until I release them onto a page.

As the night passes 10 o'clock, there's a code in one of the other units and I listen as the chatter passes back and forth on the radio. It sounds like a code Foxtrot in the unit next to mine, although no details are passed over the airwaves. Fights between cell mates are fairly common, occurring maybe once or twice a week. The issues range anywhere from a disagreement over what to watch on TV, a bowel movement after lockdown or even something as trivial as eating too loud.

The code is stood down about 10 minutes later and the sup calls me a short time later, asking if I have a spare cell. I check the muster and find nothing available, one cell offline due to having no running water. She thanks me and continues her hunt at other units across the prison.

It's a fairly easy shift and for once, am happy to have a triple go by with relative ease. There's one final buzz up just after 5 from my toothache guy and he's dealt with the same way as previously, the nurse happy to give him a house call.

When staff finally turn up an hour or so later, I practically skip out of the unit, knowing that I have 6 whole days to myself. Although night shifts can be hard on the body, officers tend to look forward to them, knowing there's almost a full week off after them. A whole week's holiday as part of your roster.

Today was an awesome shift.

Monday, November 26

Back after a whole week off and my inbox is filled with almost 400 emails. I try and get through the bulk of them before I head to my allocation today, which is in the prison kitchen. I don't mind the kitchen so much, the place running more like a place of employment as opposed to a prison unit.

If you can look past the prison uniforms, the knives all chained to the benches and the metal detectors used to scan everybody out, then you could be forgiven for mistaking it for a civilian place of work.

Because the kitchen begins long before the prison is unlocked, my 3 offsiders and I have to go around to each of the units to collect our workers. There's a list of names to carry and we split into two teams, each visiting four units and bringing a total of 22 prisoners to work. The process takes about half hour and all the cells we crack have ready and waiting workers inside.

Once back in the kitchen, the prisoners start by getting into their work attire while one of the civilian chefs makes everyone breakfast. One of the huge burners is turned into a lavish breaky buffet, frying up bacon, eggs and mushrooms. The fryers have hash browns cooking and there's juice available on one of the benches. We tuck into the food for a good 20 minutes and then begin our shift in earnest, the crew preparing to create several meals at once.

The kitchen has been known to turn over staff quite regularly due to the temptations it holds. Crooks can't seem to help themselves, often attempting to steal some delicious treats any way they can. I've personally caught several, notably one guy that tried to hide almost a dozen or so sausages down the front of his pants, the evidence clearly visible. Some have tried to steal coffee rations by hiding them in their mouths, or sugar rations up the butt. In any case, the enticement just proves too great for some and so the working crew has quite a regular turnover.

The crew works diligently until lunchtime and once we finish with our 12 o'clock muster, release the workers to eat, the civilian chefs again cooking a pretty decent meal of fish and chips. I did notice one particular prisoner repeatedly go to the bathroom but checking on him showed nothing out of the ordinary.

Once lunch is finished, everyone returns for the afternoon stretch, the planned dinner that day being spaghetti bolognaise. A huge vat filled to the brim with the sauce smelt amazing, almost to the point where I wanted to try some. But I've always had a rule when it came to prison food. I know that some people believe prisoner's food to be the best because no one would dare mess with it, but I figured you just never know.

The shift continued into the late afternoon, the kitchen a hive of activity in every corner. People were starting to assemble the unit trolleys, filling the shelves with large containers of the various meals on offer. The bulk of the meals were the spaghetti bolognaise, but there were also vegetarian salads and some kind of curry thing.

As I stood watching the team prepare the bolognaise containers, something caught my eye from near the back of the work area. There was a long row of unit trolleys, each standing with their doors open and shelves empty, waiting for the trays of food to be placed inside. Each unit required a set number of trays and several crooks were in charge of preparing the trays while others placed the trays inside.

I was standing in one of the offices and the window looking out was quite tinted, preventing anyone from outside to look in. As I stood watching over the kitchen, I noticed the crook that had been actively back and forth to the bathroom throughout the day. I could tell he was up to something because he was doing something with his hands and all the while looking around to make sure no one was watching him. I couldn't quite make out what he was doing because I could only see him from the chest up, the trolley nearest him covering the rest of him. He was preparing the sauce trays, ladling the bolognaise into trays and then putting a lid on while another crook would come and take the tray and walk it to a trolley.

It was while the crook was walking the tray to the trolley that the other one was doing something. The only way I could really see what he was up to was if I exited the office, walked out through a side door and circled to the other side of the building. There was another door almost directly behind him and although hardly used, could provide a viewpoint if I was careful.

I did just as I said, quickly running to the other side of the building undetected. The windows that lined the walls of the kitchen were set too high to look out of so I knew I wouldn't be spotted. Once at the far door, I quietly put my key in the lock and slowly turned it, carefully trying to remain as quiet as possible.

It worked and I cracked the door ever so slightly, no one inside the wiser. The prisoner who I'd been watching had his back to the door and a large rack of clean trays blocked the door from the rest of the kitchen. I watched him continue with his job, looking like he was doing everything right.

As soon as he filled a tray, another crook came with a lid and popped it on, then walked it to one of the trolleys and checking it off his list. And then without warning, while the other crook was walking the other way, the prisoner with the ladle, Sam I think his name is, slips his hand down the back of his pants and rummages around for a bit. He then spoons some more sauce into his current tray and then for some reason runs his hand through the sauce, the hand that he just had down his pants.

I'll be honest with you, I thought I was about to uncover a secret drug distribution network, my mind racing almost as fast as my heart. I watch as he jams his hand down his pants again and again, each time running it though the sauce and then wiping his hand on a towel to clean it. The other crook returns, waits for the tray to be filled and then takes it to another trolley, seemingly unaware of what was happening.

But just as I think I've seen enough to warrant closing this little cartel down, Sam does something that changes everything. He jams his hand down the back of his pants, rummages around for what seems like forever and then removes it. But instead of running his hand through the new tray, he brings it to his face and smells his fingers. I can see the brown stain of shit on one of them and then watch as he plunges the fingers into the tray. I suddenly realize what he's been doing and no longer keep quiet. I open the door, charge through and knock over a couple of the trays, the crash sounding deafening in the small space. The other crooks in the area turn to see what was happening and Sam finally becomes aware of my presence, a goofy grin on his face.

"What the fuck are you doing?" I shout, which brings my colleagues rushing over. Everyone is standing still, waiting for someone to enlighten the crowd.

"What?" Sam asks and I shake my head.

"Do you know how long I been watching you? I've seen everything." I turn to a couple of the civilian chefs that were still working nearby, unfazed by the ruckus. I wave them over and when they get close, point at the tray of sauce. "This bloke's been sticking his fingers in his arse and then wiping it through the sauce." Every set of eyes suddenly turn on him, the prisoners glaring at him with rage. Sam simply looks at the floor, the same stupid grin still smirking at us.

"Why?" the chef asks but there's no answer. One of my offsiders cuffs Sam while another calls the sup. One prisoner spits at Sam as he's walked past and he begins to laugh while another tries to take a swing. When it comes to prisoners, there are 2 things you never ever want to mess with; their medication and their food. Several begin to shout at him but he's not listening, walking briskly as he's led away.

The chef begins to rip the trays from the trolleys, telling crooks to dispose of the lot. They begin to empty the trays while several are tasked with beginning another meal from scratch. They are forced to cook fish and chips, the only other thing available at such short notice.

As I return to the office to write my report, I suddenly think back and wonder whether Sam had been doing the same thing for previous meals. Just as I approach one of the chef's, a prisoner approaches me.

"He's got diarrhoea, boss. He's my cellie. I told him not to come today but he insisted."

"Why would he do that?" I asked, pointing at the trays waiting to be emptied.

"He had a fight with a few of the boys yesterday. Maybe he wanted to get 'em back." I thank the prisoner and head to the chef, asking where Sam had worked for the lunchtime meal. He tells me that Sam was helping fill the trays of salads that went out to the units and it's enough for me to contact several units.

Four out of the seven units I call have a couple of ill prisoners, most with diarrhoea. I call the nurses and although they tell me that the effects can take days to take hold, agree to start monitoring for symptoms.

Sam was taken to Murray North and locked down, pending an investigation. Camera footage showed that he also tampered with some of the lunchtime salad trays but not all. Although they couldn't identify the specific units, the salads did make it to 9 units according to the footage.

By the time our shift ended and we were heading out, 9 prisoners were suffering symptoms of food poisoning, 1 transferred to the medical wing for observations. Although it could have been much worse, the cases were relatively isolated and thankfully contained to the trays of salads. I knew there was a reason why I didn't eat prison food and this just confirmed it for me.

Today wasn't a very good day.

I came in for a shift in the kitchen again but was sent to the medical wing instead. There had been several more cases of food poisoning overnight and one of the regular officers had to escort an ambulance into town. I didn't mind, the unit one I quite enjoyed working in. And to my surprise, Meagan was sitting in the station as I came through the airlock, grinning from ear to ear.

"Someone looks happy," I said as I came around to her side and she nodded enthusiastically.

"Can you keep a secret?" she asked and I looked at her curiously. "No, seriously. Can you?"

"Yes, of course," I replied, trying to sound serious. She paused, looking at me with eyes that seemed to try and decide if I were being truthful.

"I'm leaving," she whispered, looking around to make sure no one was eavesdropping.

"Leaving? Like going sick?" I asked.

"Leaving as in I got another job."

"What? But you just got here," I said.

"I know, but I applied for the police long before this job and I've just been accepted." She sounded genuinely pleased and I was happy for her. A girl as young as she was deserved to begin an interesting career, even if it was far more involved than this was.

"Oh wow, hey congratulations," I said, giving her a hug. "That's awesome news. When do you finish here?"

"Next Thursday is my final shift. I can't wait." I was really happy for her, as well as a little jealous. Anyone leaving to start their dream job is fulfilling their life goals. I've always wanted to be a writer and for me, I hope that one day I can afford to leave this job so I can write full time. But until that happens, I'll just have to continue these books and share the experiences you can only witness in a place like this.

The unit is practically filled to capacity as we conduct our morning trap muster and once count is called correct, unlock the 9 mainstreamers for their early runout. The weather isn't too bright today and they all elect to remain indoors, sitting around and talking shit. One sits on the bike and begins pedalling while another jumps on the treadmill. The TV is on, McHale's Navy playing through an episode from yesteryear.

It's a really quiet morning, the prisoners relaxing while the nursing staff quietly go about their business. Meagan is flicking through the newspaper while I go through my emails, slowly working my way through 1200 that are cramping my inbox. Most I have already read and so delete the majority with a simple flick.

An argument begins to ensue between biker and treadmiller, both wanting a channel change on the TV. With only a single television out here, it's a tough call to make but Meagan offers to go and sort it out under my watchful eye. She tells the crooks that as there's only one TV between them, they can either decide via a coin toss or go without entirely.

Both reluctantly opt for the coin toss and once Meagan has announced the winner, hands him the remote. The loser does what so many have before him, telling the other guy to go fuck himself, before hopping off the bike and returning to his cell.

I know it's not really the excitement you're hoping for but that was the highlight of that shift. With quite a few food poisoning cases in the unit, as well as several injuries and a couple of cancer sufferers, no one is in the mood for too much action, most opting to remain in bed, trying to sleep through whatever battle they're currently fighting.

The day seems to drag for the most part, seeming to just go on and on forever. I begin to yawn a little before 4 and by 5 am struggling to keep my eyes open. I end up doing several laps around the unit, checking open doors and strolling through the exercise yard where four crooks are busy pacing up and down.

By the time our shift finally ends, I am well and truly ready to go home, thankful for another easy day. I wish Meagan all the best in case I don't see her again and she gives me a brief hug, thanking me for my help.

Today was an Ok sort of day.

Wednesday, November 28

I was rostered in Murray North today and as I enter the unit, see Chris and Salesh in the station. Salesh is a lovely man who I've seen around the place but never really worked with before. I think he's been working at the prison for a little over a year, mostly down in the factories, an area I hadn't spent too much time in personally.

"Good morning, guys," I said as I neared the station. They both wave and shake hands when I am close enough.

"Thank fuck that cretin from the kitchen is getting moved today," Chris tells me, pointing at one of the cells on the upper tier. He's talking about Sam and I ask what's been happening with him. Turns out that several prisoners have offered rewards to have him killed, he's had faeces sprayed under his door on 3 separate occasions just yesterday and the burning through the doors is relentless throughout the day.

Another 3 officers come through and enter the station; Harry, Mick and a new officer who I don't recognize. He introduces himself as Stan and he shakes everyone's hands with frantic speed then heads for the back. I look after him curiously and Harry tells me that Stan has a decent commute to the prison and normally makes the toilet his number 1 stop.

Mick and Chris take the muster sheet and start the trap count as I check the day's movements. I'm still waiting for the computer to fire up when I hear the code called on the radio.

"Code Mike, Murray North." I look up and see the boys looking through one of the traps, shouting for the ligature knife while Mick calls for the sup on his radio. He requests permission to crack the cell and once the door is open, disappears inside while me and the others begin to bound up the stairs. There's a sudden commotion from within the cell and when we finally round the doorway, are surprised to find a different scene to the one we were expecting.

The occupant of the cell, a long-termer named Dallas Lincoln, is wrestling with Mick and Chris. Chris is desperately trying to restrain one arm, blood already pouring from a gash above his right eye. There's some sort of metal bar in the crook's hand and he's desperately trying to break the arm free, his body convulsing like a fish out of water. The hand suddenly breaks free and the metal pole connects with Mick's jaw, sounding like a dull chink as hits. He yelps in pain and is thrown backwards, his head striking the edge of the toilet bowl. As I throw myself on top of the crook, I grab the pole, punch his forearm and manage to wrestle the weapon loose, still unsure of what the hell was happening.

Salesh finally ends the struggle by slapping a cuff onto one of Dallas's wrists and painfully twisting it sideways, the crook instantly screaming in pain as the metal bites into his wrist. We manage to turn Dallas over and he finally submits, holding his other hand out for us to restrain. Once he's cuffed, we walk him out onto the pier, the cheers from the other cells now sounding like a mob gone wild. I turn back and see Mick lying unconscious on the cell floor, blood dripping from the back of his head. I call for nursing staff to attend a downed officer but they are already climbing the stairs as Dallas is led down them.

Mick comes to a few minutes later and is lifted onto a stretcher and wheeled down to the medical unit. He's eventually taken to hospital by ambulance and assessed with mild concussion and a laceration to the back of his head that required 4 stitches. He also suffered a broken jaw during the ordeal.

Chris suffered a fractured eye socket and a broken finger, the finger breaking when we rolled Dallas over onto it. Both officers are given several days off and both return to work the following week.

As for Dallas, he'd been wanting a transfer to another prison, one where his 2 brothers were being held. Because the department of corrections had denied him on several occasions, he decided to initiate a move himself, knowing that by striking an officer, the move would be automatic. He'd pretended to hang himself, tying a torn bedsheet around his neck and then sticking the other end under his mattress. He could hear the officers' approach and then held his breath, turning his face blue and then simply waited for them to crack the door.

Dallas was eventually transferred out of the prison later that day. But he wasn't sent to the prison he wanted to, instead facing charges much more serious than the ones he was in for. He was being held on remand for breaching a restraining order. Now he's facing several assault charges, the sentences of which could run into years.

The only other excitement from today was when Sam finally transferred out of the unit. The 55 crooks that lined the bottom and top tiers all began to cheer under their doors, calling for the dog to be killed. Although Sam was still wearing the same goofy grin he had when I first caught him, the colour now flushing his cheeks told a different story. He was scared, the fear clearly showing in his eyes. He knew that it didn't matter where he went; this episode was going to follow him for a long time to come.

As for the rest of our shift? We ended up receiving 2 new officers for the remainder of the shift. Movements had been suspended for the day and that left all the crooks in their cells for the most part. Several were still allowed out to make their allocated phone calls but other than that, the unit remained locked down.

When we walk out at the end of our shift, I remind myself that any shift you can walk out of the prison under your own steam, is a good shift. But a couple of my friends were hurt today, and that can never be a good thing.

Today was not a good day.

Was called in for overtime today and after the stress of the previous shift, am grateful to be given a role in the gymnasium. It's the first time I'm ever stationed in there and feel like a fish out of water from the onset.

My offsider is Kate Hunter, a 7-year veteran and also a personal trainer outside of the prison. She's been running the gym for almost 2 years and loves her job. She greets me with a warm smile when I come through the door and shows me where to stow my gear. After a few basic pleasantries, she shows me the list of activities for the day and I'm surprised that physical activities aren't among them.

The gym will be used as a make-shift holding yard for the day as a couple of units are being given the once-over. Normally, ramping a unit means searching every single cell, nook and cranny that a unit has and locating all the things crooks hope to keep. The unit is emptied of prisoners and brought to the gym where we will supervise them until their unit is cleared for their return.

Within 20 minutes, the gym is filled with 80 crooks, all jostling for cups of coffee, gym equipment and the toilets in one endless and noisy parade. We have to replenish the coffee, sugar and milk supply repeatedly until we finally call it quits, knowing that most of it is ending up in the pockets of the more selfish in the group.

The crooks keep busy with shooting hoops at one end of the gym, congregating into little scattered groups and chatting, or using the gym equipment that's spread around the outside of the hall. When their units are finally finished, they are led back out through the doors and down the corridor to home.

The process repeats four times, four units targeted this particular day. They are Tambo East and West, Thomson east and Avoca.

Units are chosen either at random or based on intel that's been received. Intel can come from officers, prisoners and civilian contractors that may have come into some information.

But ramping of units is a very good thing, often uncovering a vast array of contraband which will ultimately lead to a safer environment for all. As the prisoners are taken back to their units, those that have had things found in their cells, are separated and then interviewed plus given the opportunity to own up. If warranted, most will face a governor's hearing where the punishment will be handed out, most of it kept in-house.

I check my emails just before the end of shift and find a new one, sent moments before. It's from the Governor, thanking everybody involved for a job well done. He says that the search was deemed a complete success, having been initiated after the intel unit had received some key information regarding the influx of contraband.

Found in the four units were-

14 home-made shivs

32 x pills (14 in one cell)

3x make-shift tattoo guns

4x bottles of home brew

1x cell phone

3x cell phone batteries

The ramping proves to be a very successful undertaking and I'm always grateful to see the shivs confiscated. I know that there are always some missed and there will no doubt be more made to replace the ones removed. But it's a start and one I'm always happy to help with.

As I walk out of the prison that evening, I look forward to a long weekend with my family, happy to be walking out under my own steam. It has been another eventful month and wonder just what the next one has in store.

Today was a great day.

Author's Note

This marks the completion of my 6th book in the series and proof that these books are far more popular than I ever had imagined when I first began, and for that I thank you personally. There are several other projects that I hope you would consider, each further exploring my experiences in maximum-security.

I'm currently working on an off-shoot series, titled "Prison Days: Inmates" that I hope to begin releasing next month. These books will focus on specific prisoners that I have had dealings with and I believe their individual stories will shock and surprise you.

The other new project I am hoping to begin is another new series called "MAX". This series will be a fictional one based in a maximum-security prison but will be as true to real-life as I can make it. Think "Orange is the new black" but set in a men's jail.

Plus, I'm also working on the second instalment to my first novel, "The Final Alibi" released last month.

As you can see, I'm really pounding the keyboard trying to keep you entertained. I hope it's working for you and look forward to hearing your thoughts on my Facebook page at https://www.facebook.com/prisondaysauthor

Don't forget to subscribe to my website at www.booksbysimonking.com for all the latest updates, announcements and give-aways.

Thank you again for your continued support.

Simon

Printed in Great Britain
by Amazon